Draw Water
and Other Things

Linda Nissen Samuels

with illustrations by Irene Malvezi

Sigel Press

Sigel Press
51A Victoria Road
Cambridge CB4 CBW
England

4403 Belmont Court
Medina, Ohio 44256
USA

Visit us on the World Wide Web at www.sigelpress.com

First published 2011

Cover, internal design and illustrations by Irene Malvezi

British Library Cataloguing-in-Publication Data
A catalogue record for this book is available from the British Library

Typeset in: Chewy Blossom and Stone Sans Sem ITC TT

Printed and bound by: Bishops Printers Ltd

The publisher's policy is to use paper manufactured from sustainable forests.

About the Author

Linda Nissen Samuels was born in South Africa where she earned a Fine Arts degree with honours. She later settled in the United Kingdom.

A teacher for 25 years, as well as a prolific artist, Linda has exhibited at the Royal Society of Marine Artists and *The Sunday Times* Watercolour competition in the Mall Galleries. Many of her pupils are successful artists and designers. Her exclusive greeting cards for the international charity, WaterAid, have raised substantial sums for the organization.

Linda exhibits frequently in France and has won several awards at the International Grand Prix of Art in Cannes, winning her second Gold Medal in 2009. Her four passions are her family, painting, teaching and the light and landscape of Southern France.

To learn more about Linda, visit www.nissensamuels.com.

About the Illustrator

Irene Malvezi was born in Brazil and now lives and works in England. After qualifying at The Surrey Institute of Art and Design with BA Honours in Graphic Design, she has spent much of her professional career on technical design, illustration and photography for highly prestigious companies including The Royal Collection, Bloc Eyewear and Veritas Gifts (Corporate Luxury Accessories). She met Linda Nissen Samuels while exhibiting her work at "The Untitled Artists Fair" in Chelsea, London, and was immediately captivated by Linda's ideas for *Draw Water and Other Things*.

To learn more about Irene, visit www.irenemalvezi.co.uk.

iii

Preface

For Children and Grown Ups Alike

This book is designed for anyone from 5 -105. The aim is to aid the new artist by developing the key skills of the art of drawing.

From easy step-by-step drawings with simple lines and circles, you, as a new artist, will learn to recognise the underlying shapes of objects. You can transfer this skill to more complicated shapes as your confidence increases.

The book also introduces the vocabulary of art, such as ellipse, vanishing point and perspective, illustrated in an easy to grasp manner.

At the end of each stage you are given the opportunity to put your new-found skills into action with a comprehensive drawing of all that you have learned in the previous chapter.

Contents

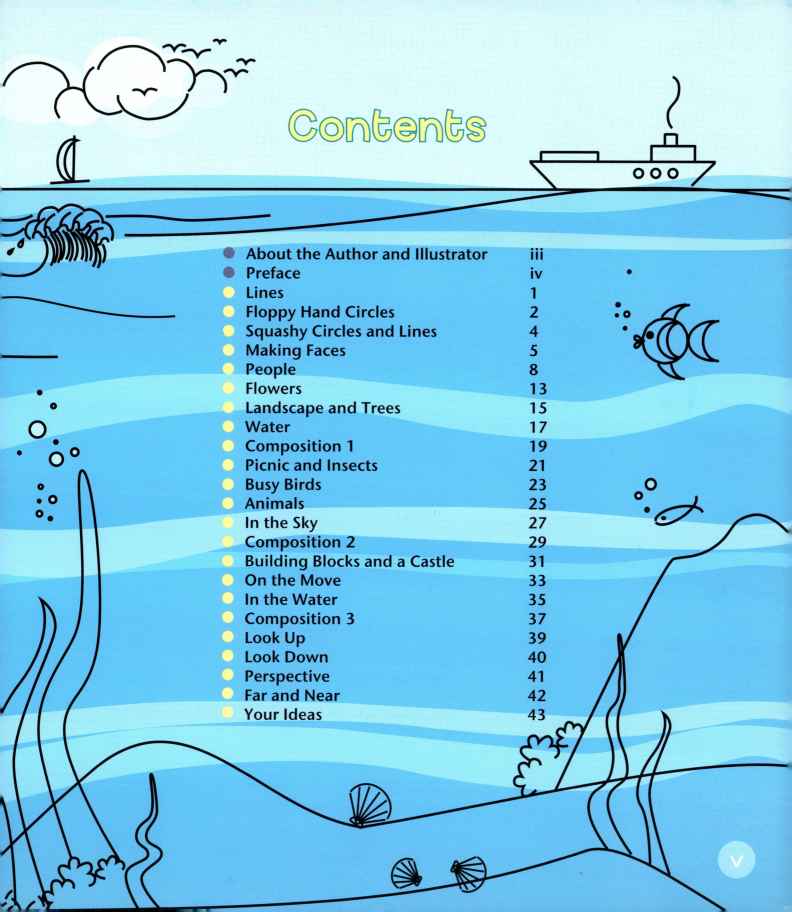

lines

Thick and dark,
press **hard.**

Thin and light,
press lightly.

If you let your pencil slide backward and forward on the paper you make straight lines.
You may use a ruler if you wish. Just press hard on the ruler so that it doesn't slip.

horizontal

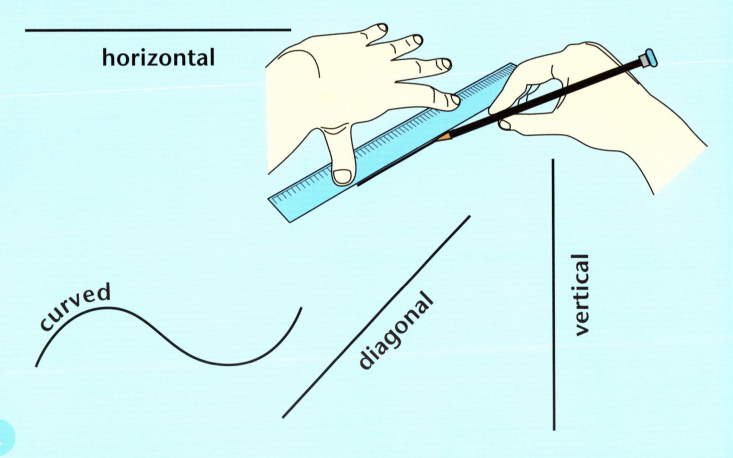

curved

diagonal

vertical

floppy hand circles

Make your hand floppy (shake it a bit). Then, hold the pencil lightly so that it almost falls out of your hand.

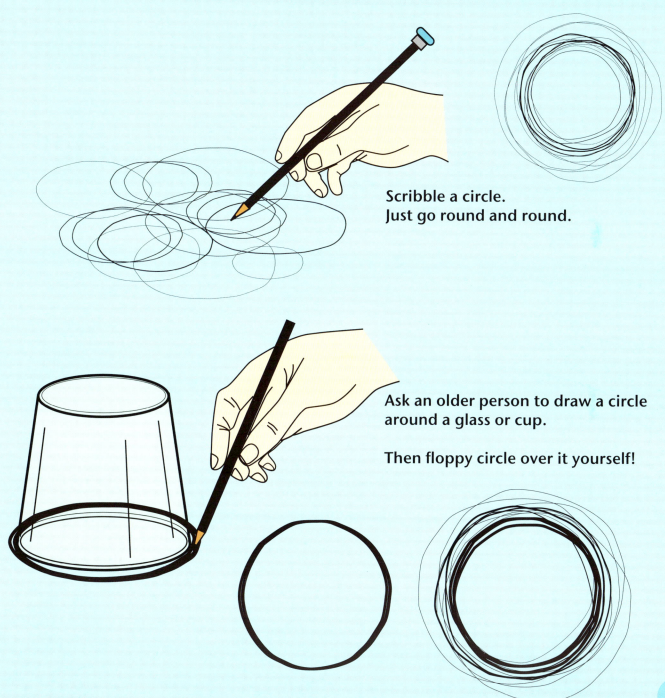

Scribble a circle.
Just go round and round.

Ask an older person to draw a circle around a glass or cup.

Then floppy circle over it yourself!

more floppy hand circles

squashy circles and lines

Squash your circle with a floppy hand. A squashed circle is called an ellipse.

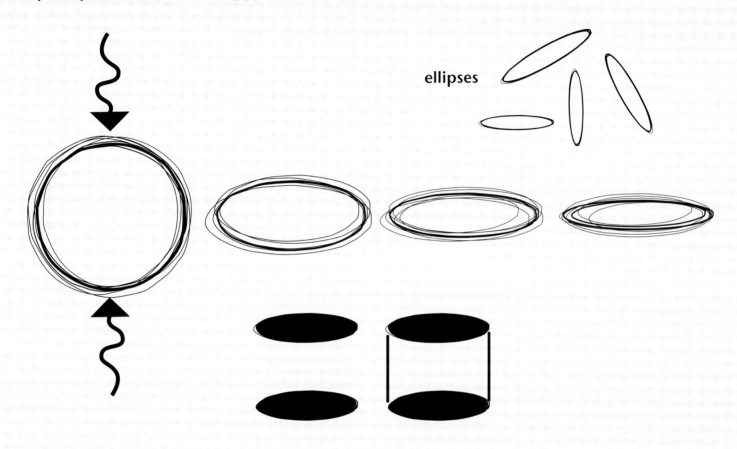

ellipses

With a mixture of squashy circle ellipses and straight lines you can draw all of these below!

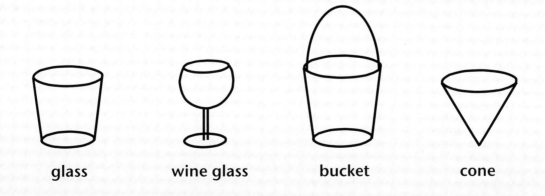

glass   wine glass   bucket   cone

making faces

5

and expressions

6

more faces

and people

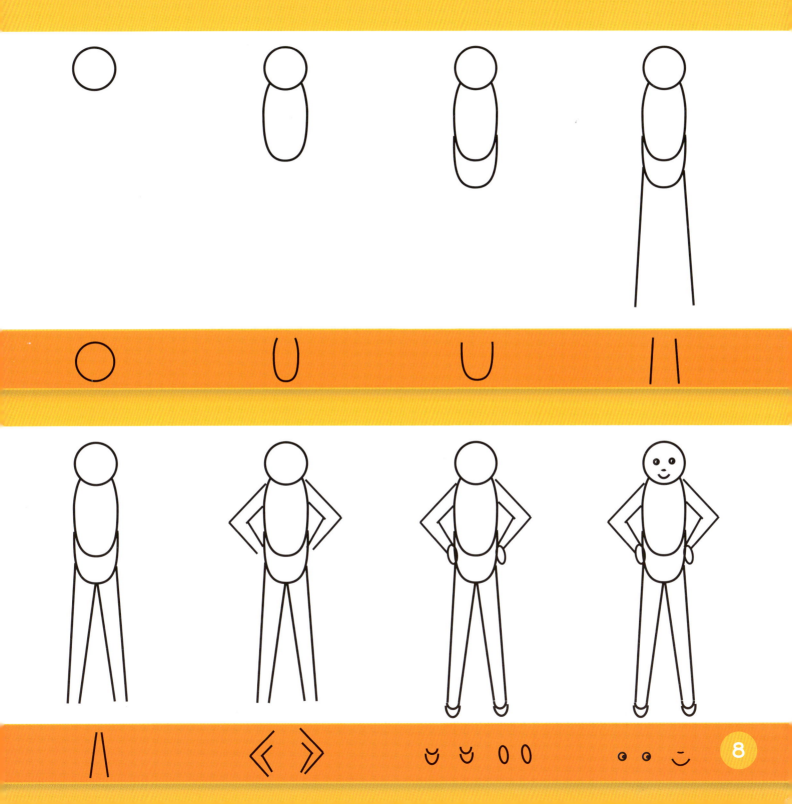

more people

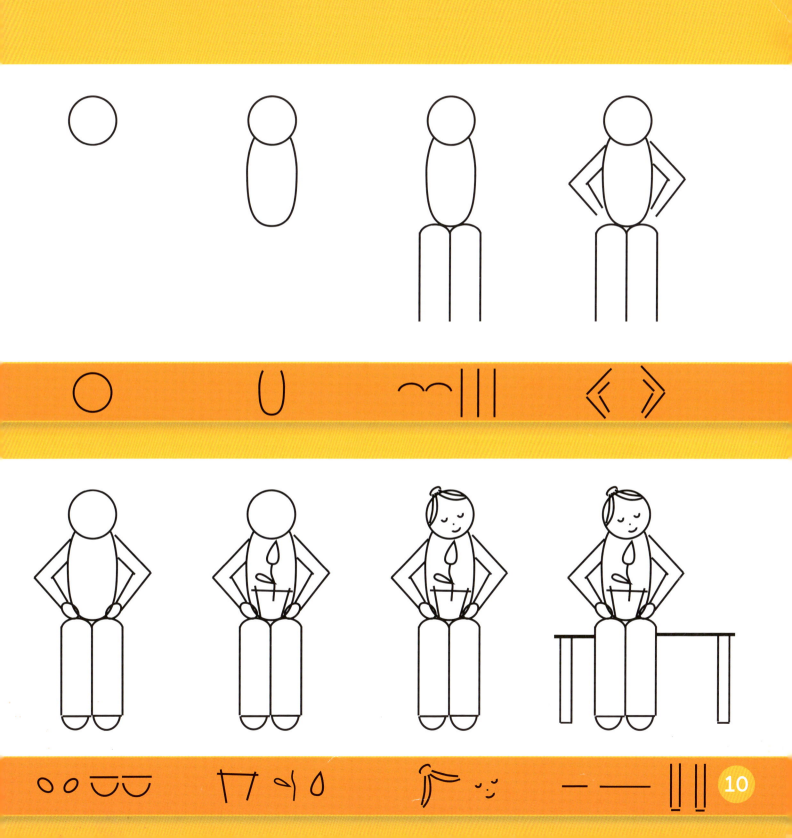

people in action

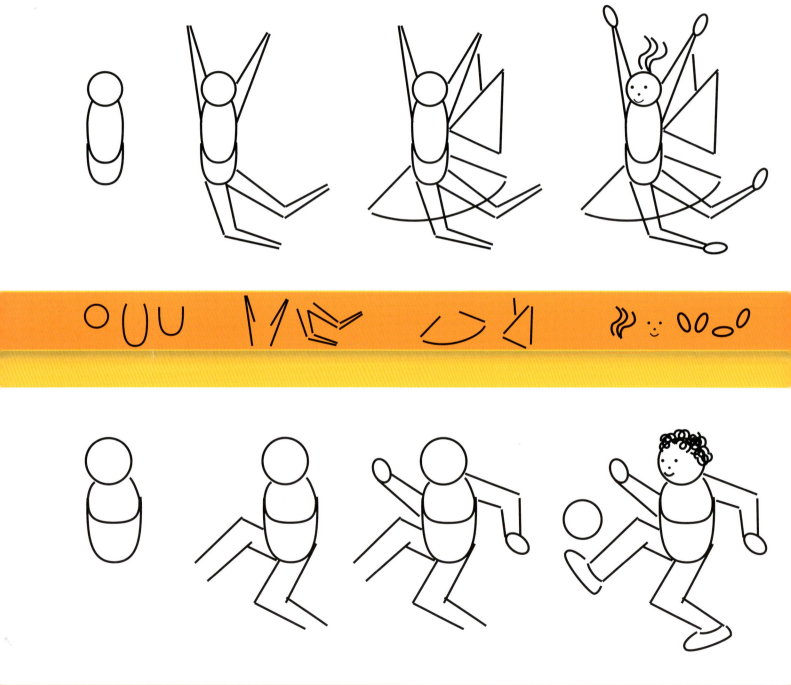

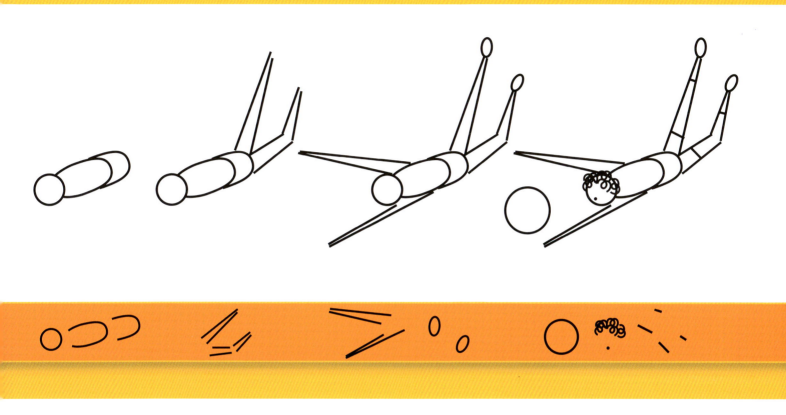

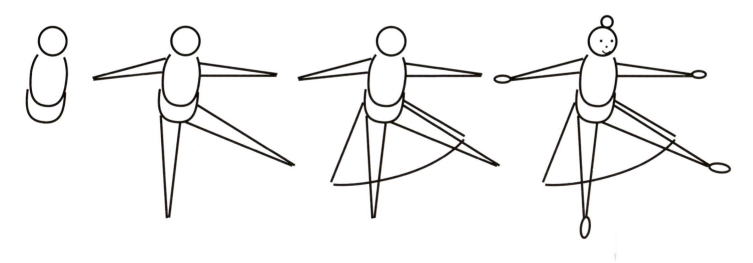

flowers

To make a petal or leaf shape, make a dot (.) with your pencil. Put your pencil on the dot, let your hand swing around and come back to the dot. Don't worry if they look different!

14

landscape

and trees

water

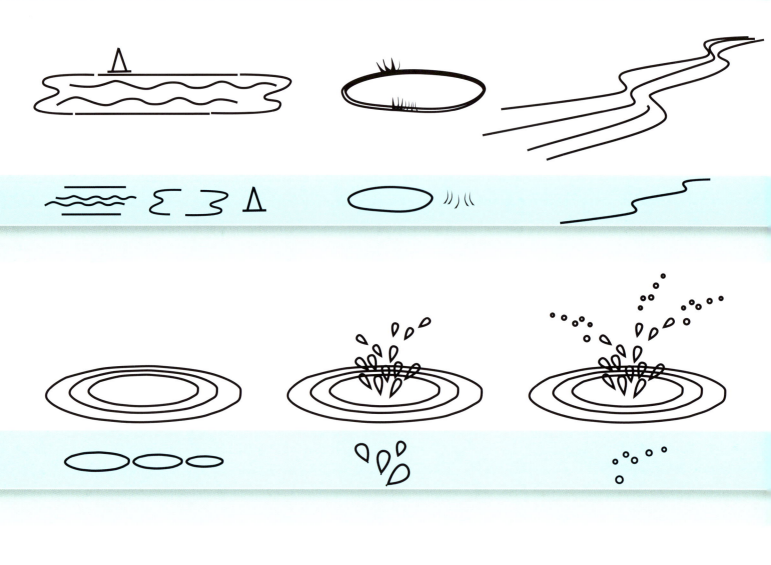

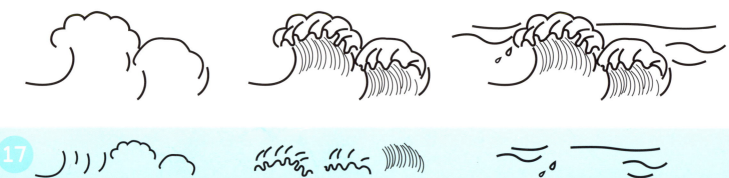

18

Now, put it all together.

picnic

and insects

22

busy birds

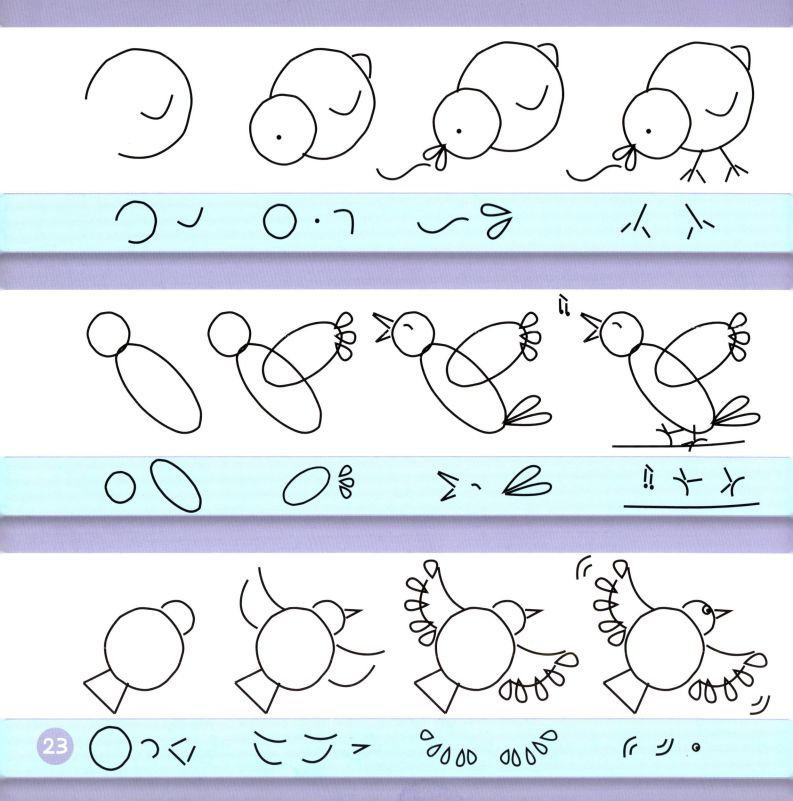

animals

26

in the sky

Just one idea. You will have many!

building blocks

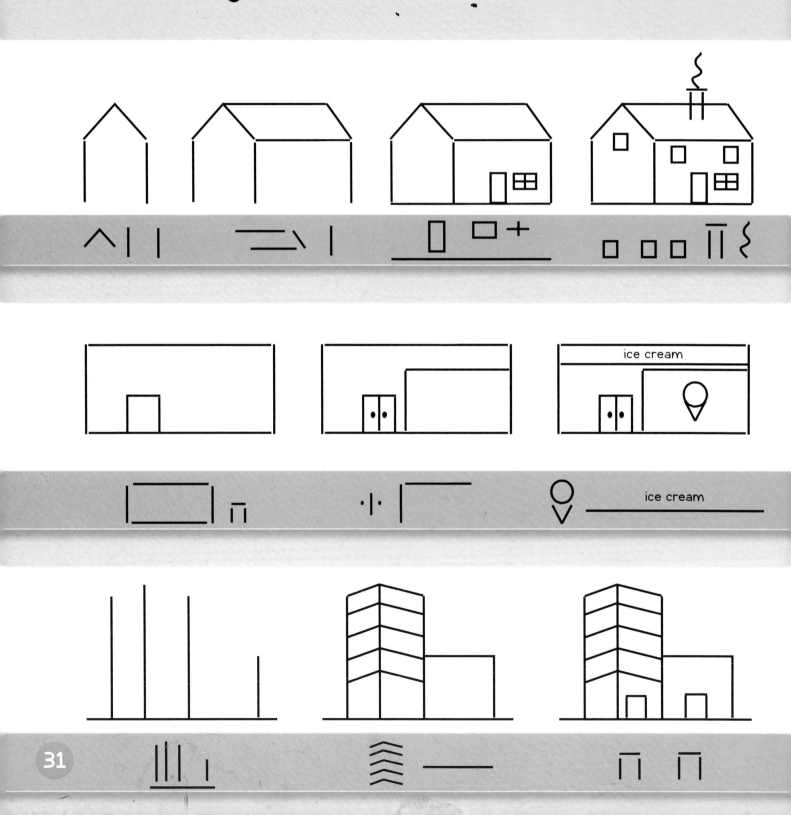

ice cream

ice cream

and a castle

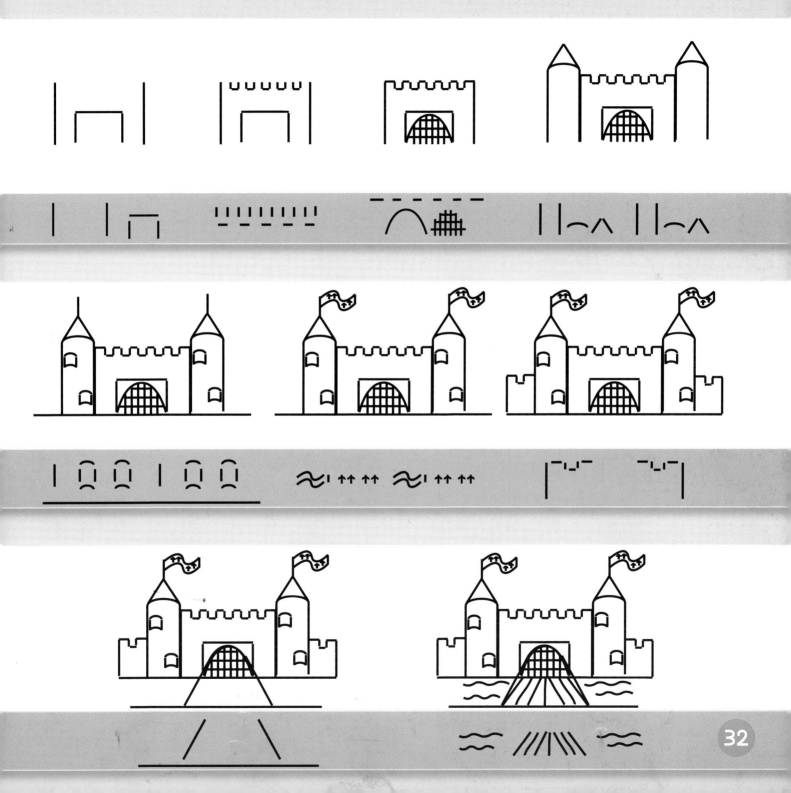

32

on the move

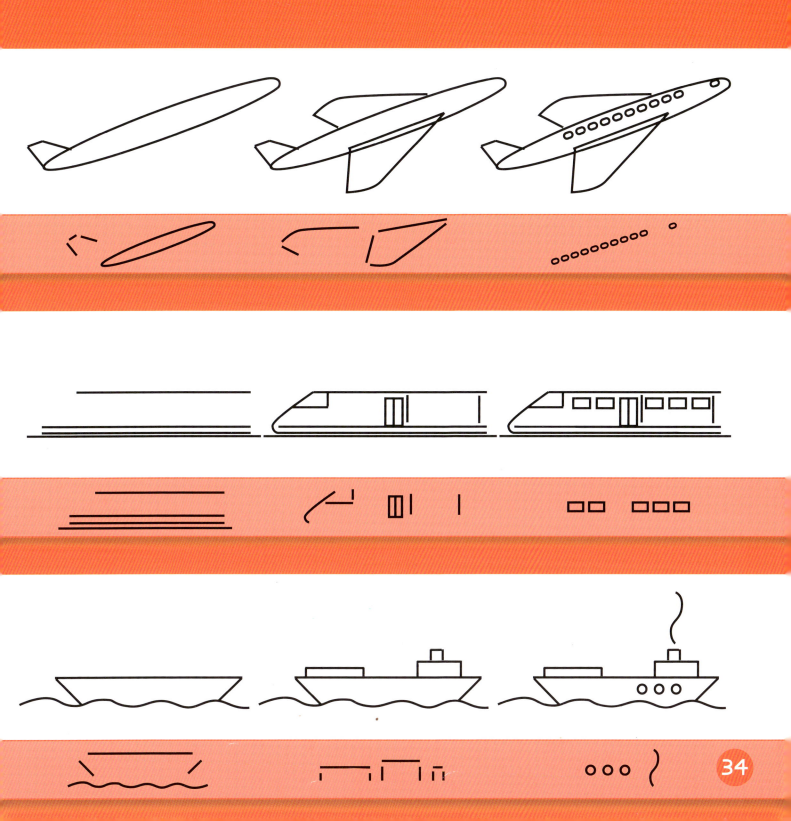

in the water

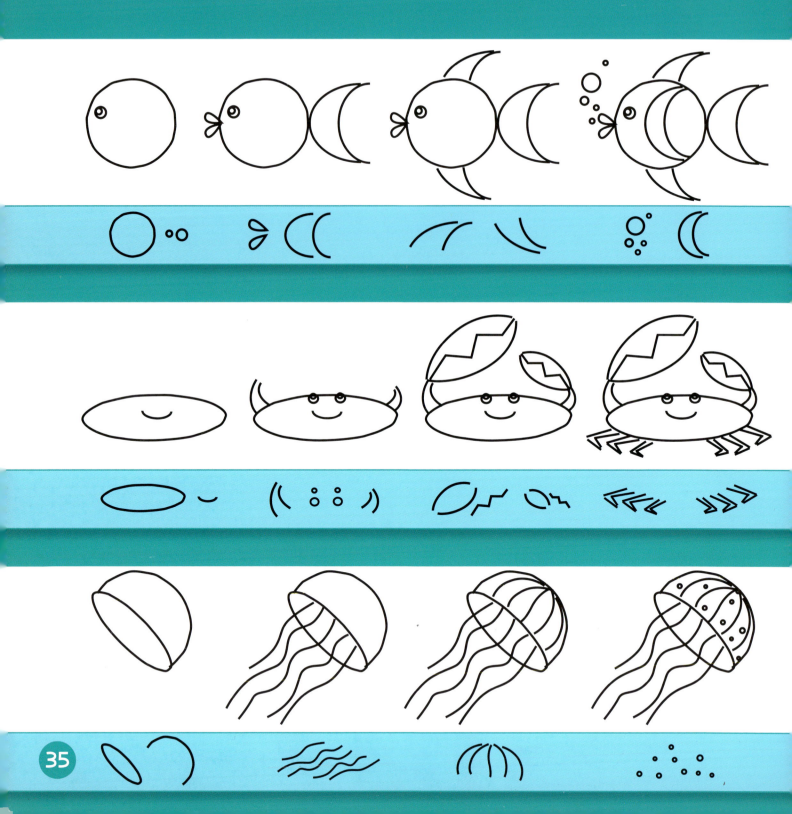

Just one idea. You will have many!

ice cream

38

look up

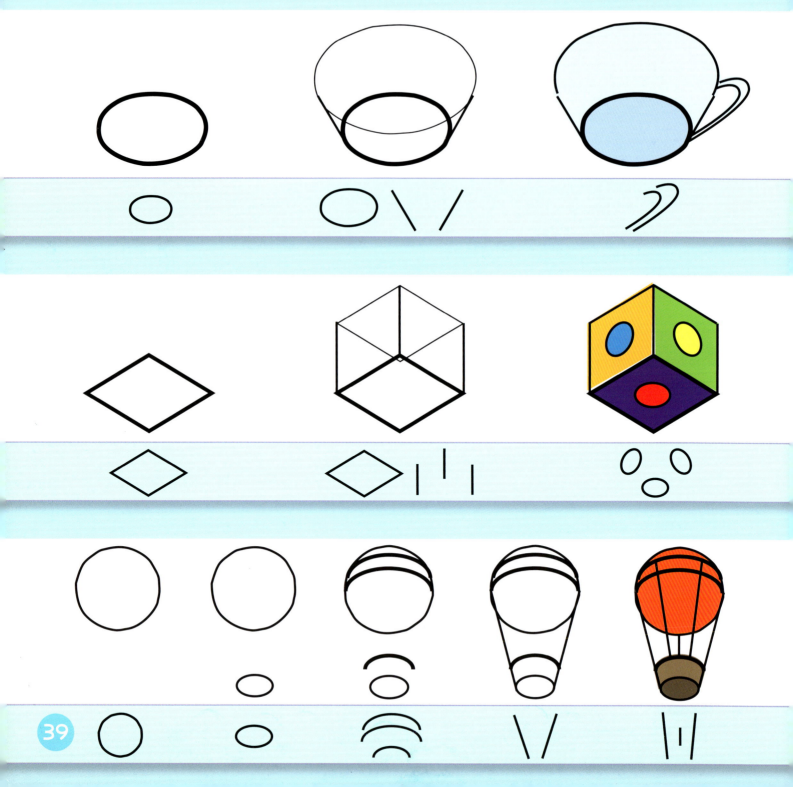

look down

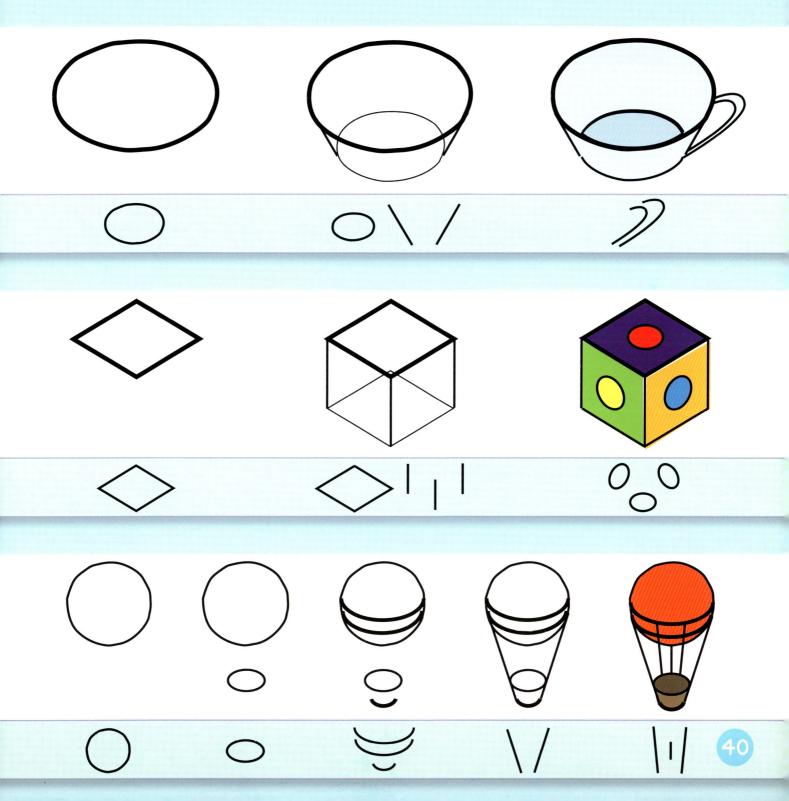

the vanishing road and perspective

The further away the road goes, the smaller it gets. Where it vanishes (Not really! It just looks like it vanishes.) is called a vanishing point.

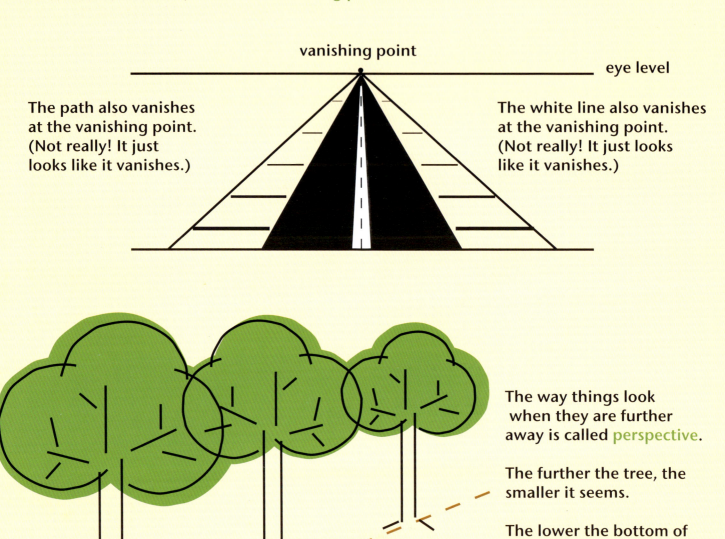

vanishing point

eye level

The path also vanishes at the vanishing point. (Not really! It just looks like it vanishes.)

The white line also vanishes at the vanishing point. (Not really! It just looks like it vanishes.)

The way things look when they are further away is called perspective.

The further the tree, the smaller it seems.

The lower the bottom of the tree, the nearer it is!

Put a flower in front of a tree.

far and **near**

Now that you know you CAN draw, take your

This book provides a few stepping stones to help you in